Our families and friends come
from many different places.
We are alike in some ways.
We are different in some ways.

WE SHOW UNITY

We work together.
We play together.

LIVING AND WORKING TOGETHER

WE LEARN ABOUT THE WORLD

BOOK 5

Senior Author
Dahia Shabaka

**Published by
Metropolitan Teaching
and Learning Company**

Reginald Powe
President

Juwanda G. Ford
Managing Editor

For information regarding permission,
write to the address below.

Metropolitan Teaching and Learning Company
33 Irving Place
New York, NY 10003

ISBN: 1-58120-829-4

2 3 4 5 CL 03 02 01

Book 5

WE LEARN ABOUT THE WORLD

We help each other.
We understand each other.
We show unity.

How do you show unity?

WE COME FROM MANY PLACES

Theo's ancestors are from Africa.
Theo and his family are African Americans.

Carmen

Carmen's family is from Brazil.
Carmen's family in Detroit
speaks to relatives in Brazil
every Sunday.

Ahmed

Ahmed's family comes from Jordan.
Ahmed and his parents visited relatives there last year.

Native Americans have been in
America for thousands of years.
Louise and her family are Navajos.

 **Where are your
ancestors from?**

Louise

The World on a Map

This map shows our world.
There are seven large bodies of land.
Each one is called a continent.
Can you point to each continent
on the map?

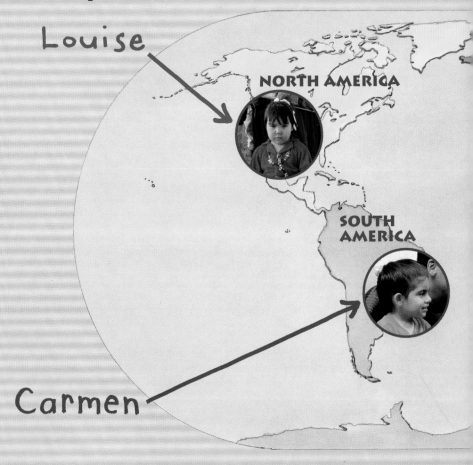

Louise

NORTH AMERICA

SOUTH AMERICA

Carmen

Look at the pictures of the children
on the map.
The pictures show which continent
each child's ancestors are from.

● Name the continent for each
child's ancestors.

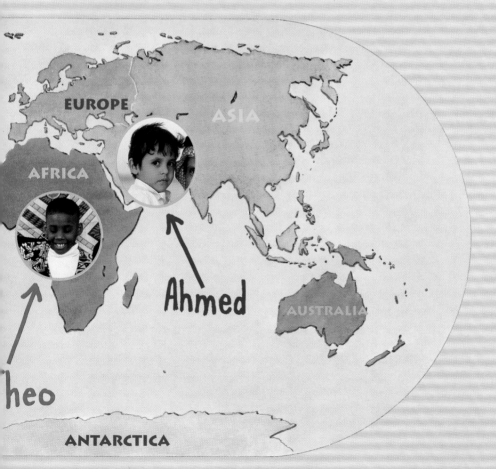

WE ARE ALIKE AND DIFFERENT

We all need love and care. People show they care in different ways.

12

We all need clothes. People wear different kinds of clothing.

We all need
to eat.
People enjoy
different kinds
of foods.

14

We all need housing.
People build different
kinds of homes.

People all over the
world say hello.

They say hello in different languages.

你好

Hola

مرحبا

नमस्ते

שלום

Selam

CHINA

MEXICO

JORDAN

INDIA

ISRAEL

ETHIOPIA

 What things does everyone need?

Your Address

Jasmine wants to send a letter to her friend Kamilah. Here is what she writes on the envelope.

1. She writes Kamilah Johnson's **name**.

Kamilah Johnson
111 Cadillac Square
Detroit, Michigan 48226

2. She writes the **number** 111 for the building Kamilah lives in.

3. She writes Cadillac Square for the **street** Kamilah lives on.

18

4. She writes Detroit for Kamilah's city.

5. She writes Michigan for Kamilah's state.

Michigan is a state in the United States.

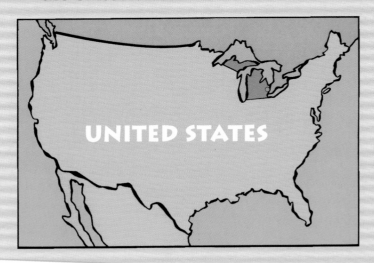

4 WE CELEBRATE OUR HERITAGE

People are proud of their ancestors. They are proud of where they came from.

We celebrate holidays to show we are proud. A **holiday** is a day when we honor a person or an event.

Many African Americans celebrate Kwanzaa.

Chinese people celebrate
Chinese New Year.
Mexicans celebrate
Cinco de Mayo.
Koreans celebrate
Children's Day.
Holidays help people
celebrate their heritage.

**What holidays do
you celebrate?**

Wrap-Up

1 How do you show unity with others?

2 Do you know people who come from other places? What places do they come from?

3 How are people alike? How are people different?

4 What is your favorite holiday? Why?